YO-EMI-666

Hope Rising

I pray that your hearts
will be flooded with light
so that you can understand
*the **confident hope***
he has given to those he called.
(Ephesians 1:18a NLT)

Day 1
Overflowing Hope

May the God of hope fill you with all joy and peace as you trust in him, so that you may **overflow with hope** *by the power of the Holy Spirit. (Romans 15:13)*

Someone told me there's one word that sums up what this year has felt like for her: **Disorienting.**

I relate. Politically, socially, economically, and relationally, we feel disoriented. The world seems chaotic and uncertain. People are stressed.

But there's something far worse than stress. Some degree of stress is normal. It's when I feel my future is gloomy and there's nothing I can do about it that I slip from stress to the real killer: hopelessness. That's what I'm seeing on faces and reading on social media posts. And that's why I'm writing this booklet. **We need hope.**

Hope involves **expectation, goals, and agency**: The **expectation** that good things are ahead. **Goals** that are compelling. And the sense that I have real **agency**, that my effort toward those goals is effective. For a Christian, hope is connected to the conviction that the same God who raised Jesus from the dead, and who will one day restore all creation, calls and empowers me for a great purpose today.

Hope is essential to surviving stressful times. As William Barclay wrote, **"A person can endure anything as long as he has hope, for then he is walking not to the night but to the dawn."** Yet today, many feel they are walking deeper into the night, not the light. You and I need to raise our hope level—not only for our own good but for the good of those around us.

But hope can't be faked.

I'll never forget seeing the Harlem Globetrotters basketball team at the Oakland Arena as a kid. During the game, star player Meadowlark Lemon doused a ref with a pail of water, then grabbed a second pail and ran through the aisles with it. We all screamed as he ran right to the end of our row and dumped the entire contents of the bucket over us... which to our delight contained only confetti!

My point: **You can only overflow with what's been poured into you.**

So what's in your bucket? Is your day filled with news reports about the latest disaster? Is your conversation full of criticism? Is your bedtime reading a source of stress? Then you'll overflow not with the clear water of hope, but with the confusing confetti of dread, pessimism, and negativity.

For at least the next 30 days, try something else. **Try filling your bucket with hope.** The Bible's all about it. There are 86 references to hope in the Old Testament. Eighty references to hope in the New Testament. Four references to it in Romans chapter 8 alone.

So for the next month, read these devotions. Memorize some of the Scriptures, pray the prayers and consider the questions. Look for ways to spread hope. Cut back on negative input (especially first thing in the morning, when you set the tone for the day, and last thing at night). You'll find that in a few short weeks you'll have a sense of calm confidence — in short, you will overflow with hope!

Question to Consider: What tends to overflow from my heart: Pessimism and worry, or hope?

Prayer: Lord, help me to have so much hope inside me that I overflow with it.

Day 2
The Science of Hope

*I pray that your hearts will be flooded with light so that you can understand the **confident hope** he has given to those he called. (Ephesians 1:18a NLT)*

Dr. Chan Hellman leads the Hope Research Center at the University of Oklahoma. In a book that inspired the title for this series, *Hope Rising: How the Science of Hope Can Change Your Life* written with Dr. Casey Gwinn, he points out, "There are over 2,000 published studies on hope. **In every single one, hope is the single best predictor of well-being.**"

He goes on to list some of the ways hope helps:

• **School:** The higher the hope of a student, the higher the daily attendance rate and the better the test scores.

• **Work:** Hopeful employees set more goals, and are better at critical thinking and problem-solving.

• **Health:** When hope is high, patients better respond to medical treatment.

• **Mental Health:** Hope is considered one of the most significant contributors to recovery from trauma.

God wants us to live abundant lives. That's why the Bible is packed with hope. When you grow your hope, you flourish.

Questions to Consider: Where in your life now do you have high hope? Where do you have low hope? Are you willing to work on building your hope?

Prayer: Lord, help me develop hope in the areas where my hope is low.

Day 3
Four Questions Set My Hope Level

Be strong and take heart, all you who hope in the Lord.
(Psalm 31:24)

When I was young, my father died of cancer. I remember reasoning, "I will protect myself from being hurt again by always imagining the worst possible outcome in life. That way I'll never be surprised when things go wrong!" And so I did. The result of so much negative thinking was, of course, negative. As I grew, I became increasingly filled with insecurity, because that's what I had been pouring into my life.

This all began to change after a major adult anxiety attack landed me in the hospital. To counter my anxiety, I put verses about the positive promises of God onto 3×5 cards and read them several times every day. Many of those verses are in this daily devotional. I noticed that each verse fell into one of four categories.

In my observation, most people tend to lose hope when they have unbiblical answers to any of these four questions:

What is my view of God?
Do I see Him as my loving Father, as my Good Shepherd, or is he a distant and hard-to-please deity?

What is my view of myself?
Am I a loser who tries but fails to do what is right, or am I chosen and empowered by God for a great purpose?

What will the future bring?
Am I only going to be disappointed repeatedly, or am I destined for greatness, promised a bright future in a renewed world and opportunities in my life now?

What is the outcome of suffering?
Is it absurd and arbitrary, or does God promise to work all things for good?

For years, my own answers to those questions were unbiblical — or at least incomplete — and so I was severely hope-deficient. But eventually, my self-talk shifted from pessimism to hopeful expectation.

In this book, we'll look at the unshakable promises of God related to each question.

If those are the questions, then here's what will change when you get hope:

Hope changes how you view God.
Hope changes how you view yourself.
Hope changes how you view your future.
Hope changes how you view suffering and death.

Does that sound good? Then prepare for a hope infusion!

Question to Consider: What are my honest responses to the four questions in today's reading?

Prayer: Lord, help me grow in hope during the next 30 days!

Day 4
Hope is Golden

*Everyone who has **this hope** in him **purifies himself**, just as he is pure.* *(1 John 3:3)*

Self-made millionaire Eugene Lang had been asked to speak to a class of 59 sixth-graders in East Harlem, New York. What could he say to inspire these students? Statistically, many of them would drop out of school to sell drugs or join gangs. In fact, he wondered how he could get these children to even look at him.

Tossing his notes aside, he decided to speak from his heart. "Stay in school," he said, "and I'll pay the college tuition for every one of you!" At that instant, the lives of those kids changed. **For the first time they had hope.**

As one student said, "I had something to look forward to, something waiting for me. **It was a golden feeling.**"

Parade magazine reported that nearly 90 percent of that class went on to graduate from high school and enter college, far above the normal rate for their peers.

Did you know that you have a similar promise? In 1 John 3:1–3, the writer explains that God lavishes his love on us, his children, with the promise of a great gift on our "graduation day" – that is to say, our resurrection. Then that great line: John says, "Everyone who has this hope **purifies** himself."

What does he mean, "this hope purifies us"? The hope of resurrection is purifying, clarifying, sharpening. If I will live forever with Jesus, and if I will be rewarded for anything I do for him in this life, that puts things in perspective. It gives me something to live for. It's motivating. It's like what those students got from Mr. Lang's offer.

When you're promised a bright future, you're inspired to endure, to do well, to say "no" to the temptations, and "yes" to the opportunities!

You too can say, "I have something to look forward to, something waiting for me." And you can inspire others with this same promise.

Hope really is a golden feeling!

Question to Consider: How does the idea of heavenly resurrection and reward motivate me?

Prayer: Lord, thank You so much for lavishing love on me as one of Your children! Thank You for the promise of heavenly transformation — may this hope purify and focus me in a very practical way here on earth!

Day 5
My Ultimate Hope

I saw the Holy City, the new Jerusalem, coming down out of heaven from God, prepared as a bride beautifully dressed for her husband. (Revelation 21:2)

Joni Eareckson Tada, who was paralyzed in a diving accident as a teenager, talks about the day she got married:

> I felt awkward as my girlfriends strained to shift my paralyzed body into a cumbersome wedding gown. No amount of corseting gave me a perfect shape. Then, as I was wheeling into the church, I ran over the hem of my dress, leaving a greasy tire mark. My paralyzed hands couldn't hold the bouquet. And my wheelchair, though decorated, was still a big, clunky machine. I certainly didn't feel like the picture-perfect magazine bride.
>
> I inched my chair out to catch a glimpse of Ken in front. There he was, tall and stately in his formal attire. I saw him looking for me, craning his neck to look up the aisle. My face flushed, and I suddenly couldn't wait to be with him. I had seen my beloved. The love in Ken's face had washed away all my feelings of unworthiness. In his eyes, I was his pure and perfect bride…
>
> How easy it is for us to think that we're utterly unlovely — especially to someone as lovely as Christ. **But He loves us with the bright eyes of a Bridegroom's love** and cannot wait for the day we are united with Him forever.

The Bible speaks of our resurrection and reunion with Christ as a wedding feast. In today's verse, the wedding metaphor is expanded to include the day all of creation — heaven and earth — is reunited with God perfectly. That day is our ultimate hope!

In this life we can live with the confidence that we're loved and accepted by the Lord just as we are. Then that day will bring about a transformation: No more struggle with sin. No more suffering. No more tears. No more loss. Reunion. Reward. Restoration. This is the great hope, to which every other kind of Christian hope points!

As Joni says, **"On that day I will dance!"**

Question to Consider: What do I know about the Bible's promises of resurrection hope for me?

Prayer: Lord, thank You for the promise of resurrection, and for the reunion and restoration and release that go along with that hope!

Day 6
The Cure for Hopelessness

Who shall separate us from the love of Christ? Shall trouble or hardship or persecution or famine or nakedness or danger or sword?
Romans 8:35

Jeff Miller was reading a book on his flight home to Chicago when he heard a muffled thump. The rear engine in the tail of the DC 10 had exploded.

As the pilots tried for an emergency landing in Sioux City, Iowa, Miller braced himself for a violent death. After the spinning landing, he found himself upside down in a cornfield, still strapped in his seat, not a mark on him, one of the few passengers who miraculously survived.

Lee Strobel interviewed Miller about that experience. Jeff told him, "I tell you the truth, it was scary, but at the same time I felt like I was **full of hope**."

Full of hope!? He continued, "There was hope if I lived; and the hope that if I died I'd be with Christ. Like it says in the Bible, what can anybody do to you if your hope is in the Lord?"

In Romans 8, Paul gives a list that sounds like the ingredients for a nightmare: Death, angels, demons, the future… yet, he says, not one of these can ever separate us from God's love. Believing this makes a difference. It did for Jeff. It means there is a place to put your fears. It means you have tools for handling disaster. It means you can sleep better tonight.

After church one day a very serious 11-year-old boy approached and said in a world-weary tone, "I am really struggling with anxiety. I hear people talking about the future, and the end of the world, and wars and terrorism, and late at night I can't sleep and I worry about all of this."

I opened my Bible to the end of Romans 8, and asked him to read those verses out loud. I could see the stress rolling off him as he read. Then I gave him an assignment: I wrote out a list of verses and asked him to write them out on 3x5 cards and read them several times a day for an entire week. He got it: "So I can replace my anxious thoughts with the truth!" I told him how this very exercise changed my own thought life.

A suggestion: Do what that eleven-year old did.

Put some of the verses from the daily readings in this book onto index cards. Read them when you wake up, when you go to bed, and perhaps at lunchtime or during breaks. Nourish your hope.

Question to Consider: How does a belief in an all-loving and all-powerful God build hope and reduce fear?

Prayer: Heavenly Father, help me to remember that absolutely nothing can ever separate me from your love.

Day 7
Hope as an Anchor

*We have this hope as an **anchor** for the soul, firm and secure.*
(Hebrews 6:19a)

There's a term used in the sailing world: "kedging." A kedge anchor is used when a ship is grounded or in rough seas. Sailors in a small boat will row the kedge anchor as far as they can from the ship in the general direction they want to move. They drop the kedge anchor into the sea. Then, back on board the ship, the sailors start the ship's winch and pull their way toward the anchor. That's "kedging."

We don't normally think of moving *toward* an anchor. An anchor usually represents the *past*. It holds you back. But as a metaphor for hope, the anchor is your future. You move toward it. In turbulent times, **you need to pull yourself into the future with the anchor of hope.**

The early Christians were anchored in this hope: Jesus not only died a sacrificial death on the cross so that we can be forgiven *now*; Jesus was resurrected, and that means one day in the *future* he will resurrect us to live in restored, immortal bodies in the new, healed heaven and earth. Meanwhile, in the *present,* we are empowered to foreshadow that day in our attitudes and actions, as ambassadors of that future world.

Winch yourself toward that anchor today.

Question to Consider: How can the idea of the resurrection pull me toward the future with hope?

Prayer: Lord, thank You for the assurance of the resurrection!

Day 8
Fear No Dragons

*May your unfailing love rest upon us, O Lord, even as **we put our hope in you**. (Psalm 33:22)*

One of my favorite places in the world is the British Museum in London. There you'll find the Rosetta Stone, the Gates of Nineveh, Cleopatra's jewelry, and something that looks like a pirate map.

It's a mariner's chart drawn in 1525, outlining the east coast of North America. At that time most of the continent was unexplored, so the cartographer made some intriguing notes: He wrote, in florid script, "Here be giants!" "Here be fiery scorpions!" and "Here be dragons!"

One day the map came into the possession of Sir John Franklin, a British explorer from the late 1700s. He scratched out those fearful statements, and in their place wrote these words:

"Here is God."

That says it all. What lies in store for you along the "unexplored coastlines" of your life — and your death? For you, that's all unexplored country, and so it's tempting to be afraid. But you can scratch out the fears and write, **"Here is God!"**

Question to Consider: If I mapped out my worries about the future, where would I write something like, "Here be dragons"?

Prayer: Lord, help me to trust in You as my Rock even when I am unsure about what my future holds!

Day 9
Hope in Who?

Do not put your trust in princes, in human beings, who cannot save. When their spirit departs, they return to the ground; on that very day their plans come to nothing. (Psalm 146:3-4)

In recent presidential campaigns, an idea has seemed to capture the imaginations of voters in both parties: The hope that we might find a human leader to solve all our woes. Pundits on both sides talk about near-messianic fervor. Of course, this isn't a new phenomenon. People have always looked with hope to charismatic, visionary, or powerful men — kings, princes, generals, revolutionaries, rabbis, popes, pastors, governors, presidents. Sometimes human leaders do great things. But it's foolish to place the full weight of our *Hope* (with a capital "H") on a human leader.

As C.S. Lewis writes: "Never, never pin your whole faith (or hope) on any human being; not if he is the best and wisest in the whole world. There are lots of nice things you can do with sand; but do not try building a house on it."

Today's verse is a reminder us that even powerful people can't save me, because they are ultimately powerless to save themselves. Only God can truly save. He *actually* has the power to right all wrongs and make all things new. And He has *already* conquered the grave.

Question to Consider: Have I ever placed too much hope in a mere human? Am I doing so now?

Prayer: Lord, help me redirect my hope away from people and toward You!

Day 10
The Hope of God's Power in Me

Now to him who is able to do immeasurably more than all we ask or imagine, according to his power that is at work within us, to him be glory in the church and in Christ Jesus throughout all generations, for ever and ever! Amen. (Ephesians 3:20,21)

Think through today's verse with me.

*"Now to Him who is **able** ..."*

Worried about whether you'll ever overcome that habit? Concerned you're not equipped to raise children? Anxious about making ends meet? God is able. Able to help. Able to empower. Able ...

*"To do more than all we can **ask**."*

I can ask for a lot. But God can do more. And He can do...

*"More than we can ... **imagine**."*

I have a good imagination! But He can do more. In fact, he can do...

*"**Immeasurably** more than all we can ask or imagine."*

What do you ask God for—or perhaps just imagine, without daring to even ask? To be healed? To find peace as you enter old age? To control your urges? To heal your relationships?

Why do we think this stuff is too hard for God? I'm not saying he'll answer all these prayers the way you want them answered—because, what's the verse say?

He is able to do *more than* we ask or imagine. His answer is, ultimately, more— immeasurably more, better, richer—than what we had imagined.

One thing is for sure: **He is able.**

After all, he was able to raise Jesus from the dead! And Paul says that same power is at work in you:

I pray that you will be able to understand the incredible greatness of His power for us who believe Him. This is the same mighty power that raised Christ from the dead. (Ephesians 1:19-20a NLT).

I am empowered by God to change, to grow, to make a difference.

Leaning into that truth brings hope.

Question: Do I truly believe that God's power is at work in me and through me?

Prayer: Lord, help me believe that the same power that raised Christ from the dead is at work in me today!

Day 11
How Do I See Myself?

*I pray also that the eyes of your heart may be enlightened in order that you may **know the hope** to which he has called you, the riches of his glorious inheritance in the saints, and his incomparably great power for us who believe. (Eph. 1:18–19a)*

A friend of mine got a card with this message written inside:

> God created rivers.
> God created lakes.
> God created you, Bob.
> Everyone makes mistakes.

It's funny—but the truth is, many of us feel like a mistake.

As Larry Crabb says, "Those who have never struggled with self-hatred cannot know how crippling a problem it can be — or how stubborn. Every minor flub or major mistake reinforces the belief: 'I am bad.'"

But don't let defeat define you. Let God's love define you.

In Ephesians chapter 1, Paul prays that "the eyes of your heart" may see the hope to which God has called you. Throughout the chapter Paul outlines the things that are true about followers of Jesus:

> I am blessed *(Ephesians 1:3)*
> I am chosen *(1:4)*
> I am holy and blameless in His sight *(1:4)*
> I am adopted into His family *(1:5)*
> I am forgiven and redeemed *(1:7)*
> I am empowered *(1:19)*
> I am destined for a great inheritance *(1:11–14)*
> I am a masterpiece designed for great deeds *(2:10)*

As an exercise, **read those truths out loud each day this week**.

When the eyes of your heart see who you are in Christ and what you are promised in Him, your sense of anticipation — your future hope — will bloom!

You are not defined by your defeats.

You are not defined by your disasters.

You are not defined by your discouragements.

You are defined by what God says is true of you.

Question to Consider: Do I feel uncomfortable affirming something the Bible says is true of me? Why?

Prayer: Lord, thank You for lavishing Your blessings on me and guaranteeing my inheritance.

Day 12
Who Am I?

But you are a chosen people, a royal priesthood, a holy nation, a people belonging to God, that you may declare the praises of him who called you out of darkness into his wonderful light. (1 Peter 2:9)

Dave Roever was a soldier in Vietnam when he was burned all over his body by a phosphor grenade and nearly died. Finally regaining consciousness in a hospital burn unit, Dave felt he was worthless to anyone and without a future.

Dave wasn't alone in his room.

There was another man there who had also been badly burned. When this man's wife visited soon afterwards, she took off her wedding ring, put it on the nightstand, and said, "I'm so sorry, but there's no way I could live with you now." She walked out the door.

Within two days, that soldier died.

Three days later, Dave's wife arrived. After seeing what had happened with the other soldier, Dave had been dreading her visit. But his wife, a strong Christian with a great sense of humor, kissed him on the only place on his face that wasn't bandaged, and then said, "Frankly, Dave, in some ways, this is an improvement." Then she smiled and added, "Honey, I love you. I'll always love you. We are going to get you on your feet and out of here!"

Within weeks Dave was healthy and out of the hospital.

The difference between the two men? One word: *Hope.* Dave went on to speak all over the world, bringing to others the hope he found in Christ.

You may feel physically or spiritually unlovable. You may have even had to endure rejection from loved ones. But in today's passage, God's Word says of all those who trust in Him:

You are a chosen people.
You are a royal priesthood.
You are a holy nation.
You are a people belonging to God.
You have a purpose.

A woman emailed me: "I used to secretly refer to myself as 'the daughter of calamity.' With an abusive past and what looked like a short lifespan ahead, I thought of myself that way for years. Well, Jesus has been doing some extensive remodeling lately, and there is no place left in my soul for this kind of thinking. I am beginning to think there is a purpose for me. I need a new 'secret name' for myself." I wrote back: "How about we rechristen you 'Hope'?" She replied, "I love it!"

To this day, "Hope" is her chosen name.

Question to Consider: How closely aligned is my own self-image and self-talk with what the Bible says is true of me?

Prayer: Lord, help me to see myself and my future the way You see me!

Day 13
The Hope of Glory

*God has chosen to make known…the glorious riches of this mystery, which is **Christ in you, the hope of glory**. (Colossians 1:27)*

"People never change. They just become more of who they are."

It's an internet meme and an accepted cultural fact. "Liars gonna lie. Cheaters gonna cheat. Haters gonna hate." But as Lee Strobel writes in his book, *The Case for Hope*, if you buy into that, you're embracing a surefire formula for utter hopelessness about your future. There is hope for change through Christ.

Nicky Cruz was the leader of the toughest gang in New York. He grew up hopeless and hate-filled after a childhood of abuse at the hands of both parents.

"I wanted to do to others what my mother did to me," Nicky says. "I used to say I felt good when I hurt people."

But when he was alone, he didn't feel so good. "Privately, when I was alone, loneliness became like a monster that crawled inside my chest and ate me up. I was twisting and fighting; I felt so lost."

Only two people claimed to see into Nicky's heart. "A counselor told me about five times. 'Nicky, you are walking straight to jail, the electric chair, and hell. **There's no hope.**'" A pastor named David Wilkerson saw the darkness in Nicky's heart, too. But he risked his life to tell Nicky **there was hope**.

"He told me: 'God has the power to change your life.' I started cursing loud," says Nicky. "I spit in his face, and I hit him." Wilkerson answered, "You could cut me up into a thousand pieces. Every piece will still love you."

Nicky and his gang showed up at one of Wilkerson's services. One by one, they gave their lives to Christ. Finally, Nicky himself turned to Jesus, drawn by the hope of a changed life. That day a change did begin in Nicky; today this former gang member is himself a minister to the gangs of New York.

Nicky knows best what they need most: Hope.

Nothing in Nicky Cruz' background would have given anyone hope that he could change. **His only hope was in Christ, "the hope of glory."**

When you open your life to Jesus Christ, you begin to see his power at work inside you, changing you. He forgives your sin and then begins to transform you from the inside-out. Those changes foreshadow that day when, at the resurrection, you will be changed completely, transformed into the image of Christ. Theologians have a word for that: "glorification." As in, *your* glorification. That's why "Christ in you" is "the hope of glory."

Faith in Jesus doesn't just mean you get a do-over.

It means you are remade.

*In his great mercy, God has given us **new birth** into a **living hope** through the resurrection of Jesus Christ from the dead. (1 Peter 1:3)*

Question to Consider: When I speak to myself, am I more like Nicky's counselor ("I'll never change!"), or Pastor Wilkerson ("I can do all things in Christ!")?

Prayer: Lord, thank You that there is hope for me as I put my trust in Christ!

Day 14
Ex Nihilo

In the beginning God created the heavens and the earth.
(Genesis 1:1)

Here's a mind-blower: God created everything that ever existed out of *absolutely nothing*.

He didn't start with a blank canvas, or lump of clay, or a sheet of paper. There was *zero* for Him to work with.

Theologians have a Latin name for this: *ex nihilo,* which literally means "out of nothing". He creates something where there was nothing.

This is a kind of creative power I cannot fathom, because we always start with previously existing materials to make something else. As Carl Sagan said, "If you wish to truly make an apple pie from scratch, you must first create the universe."

Only God truly creates from scratch.

This is not just limited to the way God makes stars and planets. This is also related to how God *changes you*.

God is not held back by pre-existing conditions. God raised Christ from the dead. He can do anything from scratch, bring anyone back to life, when there are no resources, no hope, nothing. God sees possibilities where no one else sees them. That means there is always hope.

Next time you look at someone—or look in the mirror—and think, "There is no hope there. There is *nothing*," remember how God likes to work.

Ex nihilo.

In the book of Lamentations, Jeremiah weeps over the sin and wasted potential of his people. All seems lost.

Then he writes:

> *I remember my affliction and my wandering, the bitterness and the gall. I well remember them, and my soul is downcast within me.*
>
> *Yet this I call to mind **and therefore I have hope:***
>
> *Because of the Lord's great love we are not consumed, for his compassions never fail. They are new every morning; great is your faithfulness.*
>
> *(Lamentations 3:19-23)*

Question to Consider: How do those words in Lamentations 3 give you hope today?

Prayer: Lord, thank You for forgiving me and loving me even though I have fallen. Thank You for Your mercies which are new every morning!

Day 15
When God Makes a Valley Into a Door

There I will give her back her vineyards, and will make the Valley of Achor a **door of hope.** *(Hosea 2:15a)*

What's the story behind that verse? In the book of Hosea, God talks about the wayward nation of Israel in a love poem, using the metaphor of marriage. He portrays himself as a loving husband, and Israel as an unfaithful wife.

At this point in history, Israel was abandoning worship of God for the idols of Baal, a cult that included ritual prostitution and drunkenness.

"She went after lovers, but me she forgot," God sadly sings. He asks the reader to imagine the emotions of such a husband — there is anger and a sense of betrayal, but there is also love, and a longing for the beautiful woman he knows is hidden beneath the debauchery. God says this is how He yearns to be reunited with Israel — and with anyone who has abandoned him for sin.

God's plan: To lead Israel away from the lush lands around the Jordan river and into the desert, the valley of Achor. The Hebrew word *achor* means "trouble."

This happened historically when the nation was booted into the wilderness by invading armies. As a people, they hit bottom. But God says that there, in the "Valley of Trouble," He will once again court His bride. "I will speak tenderly to her… and **I will make the valley of trouble a door of hope.**"

Don't miss it: God is saying *it's that very trouble itself* that He will use as a door of hope.

How many times have you prayed for loved ones, that God would show them their need of Him? So God leads them toward the Valley of Trouble. And then you want to step in and keep them from the valley!

Or how many times have you wondered if your own tough times were a sign that God no longer loved you? But in fact they're a gift of love from God. It's when we hit bottom that we hear God's voice more clearly.

So if you feel you're living in Achor, don't give up. That may be where God has led you… in order for you to find Him again.

Question to Consider: How does "hitting bottom" open my ears to God's voice again?

Prayer: God, thank You for Your love for me even though I have been unfaithful to You. Help me see the door of hope in my valley of trouble.

Day 16
Spreading Hope

*There is surely a **future hope** for you,*
and your hope will not be cut off. (Proverbs 23:18)

Management guru Ken Blanchard once led a training session for retail workers where he talked about the power of encouraging words.

About a month later, his office got a call from a man named Johnny, who said, "I was at your seminar. I'm nineteen. I have Down Syndrome. I work as a bagger at a grocery store and I liked your talk, but didn't know what I could do. Well, I got an idea. Every day I come up with a statement that's encouraging. If I can't find one in a quote book I have, I make it up. I print it out on 300 slips of paper."

Johnny said he signs them all, and the next day puts them into his customer's bags as he says, "Here is something special for you!"

After another month Blanchard's office got another call, this time from Johnny's store manager who reported, "Something amazing is happening. We always have lots of check stands open, but the line where Johnny's bagging often goes all the way back to the frozen food section. A customer told one of our supervisors, 'I used to only shop once a week. Now I shop almost every day, just to get Johnny's quote!'"

After yet another month, the manager called again and said, "This is changing the entire culture of our store: Like, when a flower was broken, we used to just throw it away. Now I watch as our clerks pin those flowers onto elderly women or little girls just to brighten their day. People are looking for ways they can be like Johnny and give people some encouragement!"

Johnny the grocery bagger is speaking words of hope that are changing his store's culture.

If it can happen at a grocery store, it can happen in your family, at your workplace, in your church.

Speak words of hope. Look for ways your deeds can spread hope, too.

Of this you can be certain: Every single person you see needs a dose of hope today.

Question to Consider: How can I spread hope through my words and deeds in specific ways this week?

Prayer: Lord, help me be a channel of Your hope to everyone around me today!

Day 17
Agents of Hope

...continue in your faith, established and firm, **not moved from the hope** *held out in the gospel. (Colossians 1:23a)*

It's always easy to find prophets of doom. Toward the end of his life, novelist H. G. Wells grew hopeless about the fate of the human race. He thought we'd inevitably destroy ourselves, having only "one thousand years more" to survive.

Former Secretary of State Henry Kissinger was widely quoted for this tongue-in-cheek remark: "More than at any time in history, mankind faces a crossroads — one path leading to utter hopelessness, the other leading to total destruction. Let us pray we have the wisdom to choose correctly."

In contrast, Christians are to be agents of hope to the world:

• Overflowing with hope *(Romans 15:13)*
• People called to hope *(Ephesians 1:18)*
• Always ready to give reasons for our hope *(1 Pet. 3:15)*
• Anchored in hope *(Hebrews 6:19)*
• As we trust the God of hope *(Romans 15:13)*

To a dreary, doubt-filled, despairing world, we can be a breath of hopeful fresh air.

Too bad many Christians I know are hope-busters who sound a lot more like H.G. Wells than the Apostle Paul. It's as if they believe it's more spiritual to be pessimistic than optimistic.

What is the gospel hope?

Read Colossians 1:15–23 for a further description of the spiritual reality that we often miss: Jesus is not only our Savior from sin; he is in ultimate control of history.

This doesn't mean I'm never sad.

Hope goes beyond mere emotion. Hope is the confidence-giving certainty that springs from believing the promises of God that, ultimately, every single thing that happens to me today will be used for good, every single wrong will one day be set right—and in the meantime I am empowered by God to accomplish great things in my life for others.

Question to Consider: How can I help others to stay hopeful?

Prayer: Lord, in a world of pessimism, help me to be a breath of hope to those around me!

Day 18
Building Hope with Words

Therefore, if anyone is in Christ, the new creation has come: The old has gone, the new is here!" (2 Corinthians 5:17)

James S. Hewett writes about his son, who was using a super-adhesive glue on a model airplane: "In less than three minutes, his right index finger was bonded to a wing of his DC-10. He tried to free it. He tugged it, pulled, waved it frantically, but he couldn't budge his finger free."

Eventually they found a solvent that freed his finger, and all was well. Hewett writes:

> Last night I remembered that incident when I met a new family in our neighborhood. The father introduced his children: 'This is Pete. He's the clumsy one of the lot. That's Kathy coming in with mud on her shoes. She's the sloppy one. And, as always, Mike is last. He'll be late for his own funeral, I promise you.'
>
> That dad did a thorough job of gluing his children to their faults and mistakes. People do it to us all the time. They remind us of our failures, our errors, our sins, and they won't let us live them down. Like my son trying frantically to free his finger from the plane, there are people who try, sometimes desperately, to free themselves from their past. When we don't let people forget their past, we glue them to their mistakes and refuse to see them as more than something they have done. However, when we forgive, we gently pry the doer of the hurtful deed from the deed itself...

Part of spreading hope to others is speaking encouraging words to them, words that build hope. This doesn't mean you have to deny their faults; it means you reveal the truth about who they are, and what their potential is, in God's eyes.

The Apostle Paul is doing just that for the Corinthians, who were undisciplined and worldly and troublesome. Yet he insists he will not see them through the filter of their past:

"So from now on we regard no one from a worldly point of view. Though we once regarded Christ in this way, we do so no longer. Therefore, if anyone is in Christ, the new creation has come: The old has gone, the new is here! " (2 Corinthians 5:16-17)

You may not speak disparaging words aloud to others, but in your own mind you still affix negative labels to them, labels that change the way you act toward them.

Think instead of God's words about those who are a "new creation" in Christ: They are God's masterpieces, created to do good works, planned for them since the creation of the world! They are blessed. Chosen. Loved. They have riches, gifts, potential. Speak those words aloud to people in your life!

I am so grateful that when I was a child living through some serious trauma, my Swiss-Italian aunt Pia would take my head in her hands and speak these words to me: "When I look at you, René, I see so much potential! I see that God has his hand on you and will do great things through your life!" I soaked those words in.

Today look for chances to build hope, not despair, into others with your words!

Question to Consider: What will I say to specific people in my life to build hope in them?

Prayer: Lord, help me encourage others, seeing them as new creations in Christ!

Day 19
Share Reasons for Your Hope

*Always be prepared to give an answer to everyone who asks you to give the **reason for the hope that you have**. But do this with gentleness and respect, keeping a clear conscience, so that those who speak maliciously against your good behavior in Christ may be ashamed of their slander. (1 Peter 3:15b–16)*

This is one of my favorite verses in the whole Bible: Always be prepared to give a reason for your hope.

I love doing mental exercises — how would I explain my hope in Christ to *that* person?

For example, when I read a blog by someone who is obviously intensely secular or even anti-Christian, I ask myself: If this blogger asked me to give the reasons for my hope, what would I say? How would I phrase it **gently and respectfully**, as Peter says, in ways they might relate to?

I've imagined starting with my childhood: "Losing my dad as a little kid made me long for a father. I finally found what I was looking for when I understood God as my Heavenly Father."

Or I imagine saying, "I was burned out by religion, until I saw it this way: You could spell religion 'D-O'. Do. Do things. But you spell faith in Christ as 'D-O-N-E'. He has done it; He has paid the price for my sins. That sets me free."

These mental exercises have sometimes turned into actual conversations, perhaps because I've been working out in my head what I might say.

Of course the conversations never go exactly as I imagined. They are always more interesting in real life, and require a lot of listening and sensitivity on my part so I can try to understand how to be respectful and reasonable to that specific person.

Think of one person who is not a person of faith: a real person, like a friend or even a celebrity. Imagine he or she asks, "Why are you so hopeful?" In the interest of always being prepared, imagine answering the questions as briefly and memorably as you can.

Question to Consider: What difference has my hope in Jesus made in my life?

Prayer: Lord, help me to always be prepared to share my hope with gentleness and respect. Please give me the opportunity this week to share my hope.

Day 20
Replacing Anxiety with Hope

*For **everything** that was written in the past was written to teach us, so that through endurance and the encouragement of the Scriptures **we might have hope**. (Romans 15:4)*

There's a lot of bad news in the world today.

Anytime there's a disaster anywhere on the planet, the media announce it instantly. You can't get away from it: A plane has gone down, hostages have been taken, a gunman has gone berserk, an earthquake has occurred, poisonous gas has spilled.

The availability of bad news is stunning, and it's not just limited to matters of international importance. I will never forget, years ago, watching TV and hearing a serious announcer intone over dramatic music via a multi-million-dollar satellite uplink: "CNN Breaking News... The marriage of Jennifer Aniston and Brad Pitt is over!"

Thanks to technology we receive so much more input than people did just 10 years ago, and this is probably why there's a level of fear and anxiety in our society also unprecedented in history. In the past, only God was able to know as much bad news as we get every day, and I think still only God can really handle it.

As an antidote, bathe your mind in the Scriptures. In today's passage, Paul says that **everything** that was written in the past was written **so that we might have hope**.

Everything? Really? How can every story about Moses or Job or Sarah or David or Samson give you hope, filled as they are with strange mistakes and sins and conflicts?

Well, for one thing, they were all flawed people who made mistakes and had doubts and argued with God. Yet He used them because He is full of grace and love.

That means there's hope for you and me too.

Questions to Consider: How do I allow God to encourage me with hope through the Scriptures every day? Do I spend too much time reading or watching things that drain my hope?

Prayer: Lord, thank You for giving me Scripture not just as a set of rules or as theological history, but so that I might have hope!

Day 21
Expecting the Best

*"You answer us with awesome deeds of righteousness, O God our Savior, **the hope of all the ends of the earth and of the farthest seas.**" (Psalm 65:5)*

In his book *Windows of Hope*, Richard Lee tells the true story of famous Navy Admiral James Stockdale. One of the first POWs of the Vietnam War, Stockdale was frequently tortured during his seven years in a prison camp.

After his release, Stockdale said the only thing that kept him alive was hope: Hope with each new day that he might be released before sundown. He knew that without this sense of daily anticipation, he would have died, like so many others without hope.

What was good for Stockdale is good for you. **Do you have daily anticipation that God will show up in your life and open doors for you?** Do you anticipate the "awesome deeds" the psalmist writes about in today's verse?

One reminder: Our culture uses the word *hope* almost interchangeably with the word *wish* (as in, "I hope I win the lottery!"). But the Bible defines hope differently: As a confident expectation that God will keep the promises in His Word.

Promises like what? If I have surrendered my life to Christ, the Bible promises...

My salvation *(Ephesians 1:13–14)*
My resurrection *(1 Corinthians 15:20–23)*
My glorification *(Galatians 5:5)*
My eternal life *(1 Corinthians 9:25; 1 John 2:17)*

My deliverance from evil *(Psalm 33:16–18)*
The Second Coming of Christ *(1 Thess. 4:13–14)*
That in all things God works for the good *(Rom.8:28)*
My special ability to do good works now *(Eph.2:10)*
...and much more!

As Richard Lee points out, if you substitute the
word *assurance* or *conviction* for hope in the list above, you
start to get the biblical idea of hope!

Question to Consider: Do I live with daily anticipation
that God will act in my life? What difference would this
make in my conversations, my relationships, my work?

Prayer: Heavenly Father, help me have hope as I start
each day that You will act in a powerful way.

Day 22
Living with Daily Expectation

This is the day the Lord has made; Let us rejoice and be glad in it! (Psalm 118:24)

One of my favorite holiday traditions is imported from our family's ancestral homeland of Switzerland: Advent calendars!

As a child, each day in December, I would eagerly anticipate opening another little paper door. At first, I'd look forward to simply seeing a new picture. Later, advent calendars changed to feature hidden chocolates or even little toys. I liked them because they spread out the Christmas joy; the thrill of opening a present touched every day, not just December 25th.

That's a lot like living with biblical hope. It fills you with expectation, not just of the ultimate Day when all your hopes will be fulfilled, but of the way God will work every single day until then.

Yet advent calendars simply wouldn't work without the big double doors labeled "December 25." Anticipating that big day was exactly what made the other, smaller advent doors so magical for me as a kid.

Again, much like biblical hope. That daily sense of expectation is made more wondrous as you anticipate the Great Day — the day of your resurrection and God's glorious re-creation of the heavens and earth.

C. S. Lewis pointed out this link:

> Hope means a continual looking forward to the eternal world. It does not mean that we are to leave

the present world as it is. If you read history you will find that the Christians who did the most for the present world were just those who thought most of the next... It is since Christians have largely ceased to think of the other world that they have become so ineffective in this. Aim at Heaven and you will get earth 'thrown in'; aim at earth and you will get neither.

Try this experiment: As soon you wake up each day this week, say to yourself, "This is the day the Lord has made; I **will** rejoice and be glad in it!"

I've been trying this and it has really changed my outlook; it reminds me each day is sort of like a little advent calendar door, with something God wants me to experience inside — an opportunity to serve, to grow, to laugh. I can miss it if I'm not looking.

Question to Consider: How can I remind myself to live each day in hopeful expectation?

Prayer: Lord, I choose to rejoice in *this* day. I know there will be "advent calendar doors" for me to open today that You place in my life. Help me live with a daily sense of expectation.

Day 23
Beyond Pessimism and Optimism

*...a faith and knowledge resting on **the hope of eternal life**, which God, who does not lie, promised before the beginning of time. (Titus 1:2)*

During his time as a prisoner of the Nazis, German pastor Dietrich Bonhoeffer wrote to a friend that he was neither a pessimist (expecting things to get worse) nor an optimist (expecting things to get better). He said that he was **living by hope**.

What's the difference?

Pessimists doubt anything good will happen.

Optimists believe only good will happen.

But a hopeful person is realistic: He acknowledges there may be immediate suffering — but ultimate reward.

Bonhoeffer knew what the early Christians knew: As long as I am alive, even in prison, God will use whatever happens to me for good (it happened for Bonhoeffer — his prison letters still inspire readers today); and even if I die, I am promised heaven... and the resurrection! When everything was stripped away from him, this hope is what remained, and what sustained him on a daily basis.

In today's verses from Titus 1:1–3, Paul reminds Titus that **our entire faith rests on hope**; specifically the hope of eternal life God promised to us. It is the only thing that cannot be taken away from us, even in prison.

Writing during the 2008 economic meltdown, Gordon MacDonald said:

God intends that Christians ask once again: "What is at the core of the real gospel that we may have forgotten during the days of prosperity?" May hopeful people relearn how to differentiate between the "city" of today and the enduring city that is to come. Such hope — liberally spread — could have revival proportions.

In times of uncertainty and chaos, I have a choice; I can surge with the crowd toward the cultural and political idols peddling a false hope, or I can double down on the real gospel, and live as Jesus did, as a person of grace, hope, and love in a world of unrest. I can choose to stare at my losses or I can fix my eyes on God's promises.

Do an honest self-evaluation: Does my faith rest solidly on the real gospel?

Question to Consider: Am I a pessimist, an optimist, or am I living by hope?

Prayer: Lord, help me today to live not as a cynical pessimist or a blind optimist, but as a biblically optimistic, hopeful person.

Day 24
Living Hope that Never Fades

*Praise be to the God and Father of our Lord Jesus Christ! In his great mercy he has given us new birth into a **living hope** through the resurrection of Jesus Christ from the dead. (1 Peter 1:3)*

I often hear Christians fretting about the latest headlines. With each new crisis, many seem to worry: "Is this Armageddon?" "Is it the end of America as we know it?" "Are we in the last days?"

Think about this: For many of the first-century believers, it *was* the end of their lives as they knew it. They sincerely believed they *were* living in the last days. Yet when you read their letters in the New Testament, what do you see?

G. Campbell Morgan was a great Scottish preacher in the time of World War II. Imagine hearing him say these words in his Scottish brogue:

> I have no sympathy with those who tell us these are the darkest days this world has ever seen! The days in which we live are appalling. But they don't compare to the days of the first Christians. Notwithstanding, the dominant tone of their letters is one of triumph; in fact, we never see them cast down, we never see them suffering from pessimism fever, they're always triumphant! If ever I am tempted to think that religion is dead today, it is when I listen to the wailing of some Christian people, "Everything is going wrong!" Oh, be quiet! Think again! Judge again! Not by the circumstances of this passing hour, but by the infinite things of our

gospel and our God! That is exactly what the writers of this New Testament did!

I love that. Read 1 Peter 1:3–9 for an example of this. The readers were suffering in all kinds of trials, yet Peter tells them they have a living hope that can never fade.

Do not stake your happiness on circumstances, which can change so quickly, but on the certain hope promised by God.

Question to Consider: How does trust in my unchanging inheritance give me serenity in the midst of chaos today?

Prayer: Lord, help me to be soaked to my soul with a sense of hope. I get anxious, and I need You to calm me down with the peace of Christ.

Day 25
When Hope Is Shattered

Against all hope, Abraham in hope believed...
(Romans 4:18a)

The famous Christian writer G. K. Chesterton said:

> Hope means hoping when things are hopeless, or it
> is no virtue at all... As long as matters are really
> hopeful, hope is mere flattery or platitude; **it is only
> when everything is hopeless that hope begins to
> be a strength**.

In today's passage the Apostle Paul recounts the story of
Abraham. God had promised that one day Abraham would
be the father of many people, but at age ninety-nine,
Abraham still didn't have any children, and his wife Sarah
had been infertile her whole life. It was an impossible
situation.

Maybe you can relate. Perhaps you're feeling pretty hopeless
in some area of your own life. You wonder: Where do I put
my hope now?

Where did Abraham put his hope? Himself? No. His
feelings? No. Positive thinking? No. He believed in
God's *promise* to him.

Positive thinking and hope are not the same thing.

Positive thinking helps a lot — in situations where you have
control over the outcome. But positive thinking is worth
little when things are out of your control. Only hope in
God's promises helps then.

Of course, God never promises He will do things the way you expect, according to your timetable. That certainly didn't happen for Abraham and Sarah!

But God promises He'll keep His word. And He promises it's when things are hopeless that I'll grow in ways I never could have imagined.

Eventually, Abraham and Sarah had a miracle baby. They named him Isaac, which means "laughter," because they had laughed at the promise of a child. But, as they say, God always has the last laugh.

Question to Consider: Where do I feel hopeless in my life right now? What promises of God can I cling to for hope?

Prayer: Lord, I confess to You an area where I feel little hope today. I claim Your specific promises that You will mold me into the image of Christ, that You will "birth" a new person in me!

Day 26
Motivated By Hope

Now faith is being sure of what we hope for and certain of what we do not see. This is what the ancients were commended for.
(Hebrews 11:1–2)

Flagstaff, Maine was a picturesque New England village with lovingly maintained homes and shops.

But in the 1940s the State of Maine decided to build a dam that would flood the valley where the village had stood for 100 years.

As soon as word spread, all repairs stopped. Week by week the whole town became more bedraggled — broken windows, littered streets, overgrown yards. Someone asked, "Why?" The answer famously came back:

"Where there is no hope in the future,
there is no motivation in the present."

Victor Frankl, a Jewish psychologist, discovered this truth in a Nazi concentration camp during World War II. Frankl began observing fellow prisoners to discover what coping mechanism could help him endure.

Here's what he found: People who could not make their present suffering fit with their faith, who could not find meaning in their worldview, despaired and eventually gave up and died. But those who could find meaning from their faith were then able to find hope for a future beyond their present suffering, and they survived.

The writer of the book of Hebrews reminds his readers of this very truth in Hebrews chapter 11. Writing to Christians who were tempted to give up on their faith because of persecution, he paints a stirring picture of the ancient heroes of the faith who braved dangers, endured suffering, and took huge risks because they had something to live — and die — for: **The promise of God that the best was yet to come.**

He says that this is the very essence of faith. Then he challenges his readers to have the same kind of endurance based on hope.

Questions to Consider: How does hope in the future provide motivation in the present? If you were in a prison like the one Victor Frankl survived, how would your faith help you deal with your suffering?

Prayer: Lord, help my hope in the future give me motivation in the present!

Day 27
Hope Gives Wings

*Those who **hope** in the Lord will renew their strength. They will **soar on wings** like eagles; they will run and not grow weary, they will walk and not be faint. (Isaiah 40:31)*

One of the greatest comeback stories in sports: San Francisco Giants pitcher Dave Dravecky's return from cancer.

When a tumor was found in Dave's pitching arm, we fans thought his baseball days were over. We were all wrong.

I still get chills when I remember August 10, 1989, the day I tuned in to watch Dave lead the Giants over the Reds in his first major league game in over a year. He received twelve standing ovations, even from Reds fans!

But in his next start, his pitching arm snapped as he threw in the fifth inning. Doctors later discovered more cancer, and this time the whole arm had to be amputated.

Everyone wondered: How would Dave respond to this setback?

He says he looked in the mirror following the surgery and prayed, "Okay, God. This is what I've got to live with. Put this behind me; let's go forward."

As he walked the hospital corridor soon afterward, he came to a lounge where a whole family sat waiting during surgery. The worried wife told him her husband had cancer.

Dave sat down with them, and her son asked, "Where do you get your peace?" The entire family listened as he gently shared his faith.

"It is hard to understand suffering in this life," he told them. "But you know, sooner or later *everything* on this earth is going to end. I believe God can and does heal people, but more important than that, I believe in the eternal hope of heaven. When I die, that's where I'm going. Heaven is my home."

The conversation changed that family, and was the start of an international ministry to cancer patients.

Dave's strength and endurance is a testimony to the effect of biblical hope. Even the most impressive people are like dandelion seeds in a breeze compared to the permanence of God. The good news is, I can find my permanent hope in Him.

It's a fact: Hope gives wings.

Question to Consider: How does Dave's story help explain the way that hope in God gives strength in tough times?

Prayer: Lord, help me to see both the impermanence of my world and Your permanence. Help my hope increase as I think of my heavenly home.

Day 28
Does Hope Really Make a Difference?

Brothers and sisters, we do not want you to be ignorant about those who fall asleep, or to grieve like those who have no hope.
(1 Thessalonians 4:13)

We still grieve, but we do not grieve as those who have no hope.

We still die, but we do not die as those who have no hope.

I had just finished speaking at the funeral of a young woman one day when one of her friends strode up to me and, in front of the other mourners, said, "That's all B.S.! Everything you said about heaven and Jesus — all B.S.! Whether you believe or not, it all ends the same, doesn't it? Doesn't it?!"

I waited until she had blown off a little more steam, and then asked, "Do you really want an answer?" She was surprised, but nodded yes.

"Then," I said, "Come with me right now, because I'm going directly from this funeral to visit two people in the cancer wing at the hospital. One is the father of a friend. He never made room for faith, and is now petrified of dying, white-knuckling his ride into eternity, gripping the side rails of his bed, staring ahead with panicked eyes. I try to speak words of comfort, but I don't know if he even hears me.

"After that, walk with me down the hall to see my friend Meryl. She's dying, too, in the last stages of cancer. But when you enter her room it's like you've walked into a serenity zone, peace perfuming the place like incense. She radiates calm confidence as she welcomes her visitors and speaks of soon seeing her Savior.

"Then — only after you have seen the difference between them — only then, tell me that it's all B.S."

She walked away, nervously refusing to go on a visit that I think might have changed her life forever.

If you ever wonder why pastors still believe after they've seen so much death as part of their calling, you need to know: **We have seen the difference that Christian hope makes.**

I'm not saying there are never moments of fear or depression for Christians facing death. Of course there are. I *am* saying, as someone who has been with innumerable people facing death, that there is a definite difference for those who believe they have hope as they head into eternity.

Question to Consider: How can I encourage myself and others today with the hope Paul speaks of in these verses?

Prayer: Lord, thank You for the promise that, ultimately, You have my destiny and the destiny of the world in Your hands!

Day 29
Get Ready, Boys!

Therefore, prepare your minds for action; be self-controlled; **set your hope fully** *on the grace to be given you when Jesus Christ is revealed. (1 Peter 1:13)*

On his infamous expedition to the Antarctic, explorer Ernest Shackleton and his 27 men encountered nightmarish conditions. Temperatures dipped to 100 degrees below zero. Their ship was caught in pack ice for ten months.

Shackleton had to leave most of his men on Elephant Island to go for help. After sailing a lifeboat through a storm, Shackleton finally reached a whaling station. Three times he tried to return to rescue his crew, but bad weather turned him back repeatedly. Finally, ten months after he had left them, he found a narrow channel through the ice. When he finally got to Elephant Island, he was amazed to find his men not only alive and well, but *already packed and ready to board his ship.*

Shackleton asked his men how they happened to be ready to leave on the very day he arrived. They told him that every single morning their leader said, **"Get your things ready, boys, the boss may come today."** That infused them with a daily dose of hope.

Today's Scripture says, in essence, the same thing: The boss may come today! So be ready. Think of the joy you'll feel. The rewards that he promised. One way or another, you'll meet Jesus one day, so be ready!

Question to Consider: How can a belief that Jesus will return to restore God's kingdom bring hope?

Prayer: Lord, help me live with daily anticipation of the fulfillment of Your promises!

Day 30
Hope Review

*I pray that your hearts will be flooded with light so that you can understand the **confident hope** he has given to those he called… (Ephesians 1:18 NLT)*

We started a month ago by posing four questions that determine your hope level:

What is my view of God? Christian hope says God loves me and plans the best for me.

What is my view of myself? Christian hope says I have God's unlimited power in me for the challenges and opportunities of life.

What will the future bring? Christian hope says I have an unshakable inheritance in the new heaven and new earth. And in this life, God has a plan for good, and not for evil.

What is the outcome of suffering? Christian hope says God will use every hard time in my life for His perfect plan, and the outcome of suffering will be Christ-likeness.

Here's my hope for you and me — the verse that started this whole experience seven weeks ago:

*May the God of hope fill you with all joy and peace as you trust in him, so that you may **overflow with hope** by the power of the Holy Spirit. (Romans 15:13)*

Question to Consider: How have I seen this emphasis on hope make a difference in my life?

Prayer: Lord, thank You for all these reasons for hope. May I overflow with hope to those around me!